Wonder

Samantha Nichols

BookLeaf Publishing

India | USA | UK

Presentation by *BookLeaf Publishing*

Web: www.bookleafpub.com

E-mail: info@bookleafpub.com

ISBN: 9789360940416

First edition 2024

Macarons

Many flavors looking back through the display
Which to choose, which to choose
Tiramisu, Madagascar vanilla, Birthday cake,
      Bubble gum
The chosen flavors

The first shared with a wide-eyed little boy
I never received my cookie back
My father, a grandfather, went and bought more
A definite number one in my four

The second eaten at home
The joy and deliciousness of the first
Showed this to be underwhelming

Almost bland throughout the eating
Will eat again

The third covered in sprinkles
Very similar to the second,
But the crunchy sprinkles made it
Beautiful, delicious, and wonderful
A definite second place

The fourth was blue
Very different to the previous three
This was choked through
Primarily due to expense
Never ever again

Rabbit

Brain twisted rot
Circling around
       And around
           And around
My exhausted body

New rabbit holes
Long rabbit warrens
O what wonders and delights
Will I find down here?

Not a wink of sleep to be had
       Eyes drooping
           Mind swooping
A poem appears in the dim light of the warren
Unfolding in front of me
Quite unlike the dreaming fantasy
That I want

Work

Walk in
Look around
Nothing is the same now

New colors
New patterns
Old faces
Warm embraces

My favorite style
All over the walls
A visitor, one who left,
And no one calls

What will we learn?
How will we look?
When do I work next?

Grading

Is this a word?
I have no idea what this means.
I say it aloud,
And now I understand.

I squint and turn the paper,
At first a slight tilt to the left
Then a slight tilt to the right
I try upside down
Then horizontally
I wonder whose name that actually is

I know we talked about this in class.
I know you JUST read this in the book.
How did you get this question wrong?
What do I need to reteach?
What vocabulary do you need to learn?
Am I a good teacher?

Rain

Above me water condenses
    And then falls
Above me the life-giving liquid
    Heeds all of nature's calls

Acidity high
    A slow death poison
Fueled by short-sighted policymakers
    Those "movers and shakers"

Why seed the clouds
    Causing floods
And misplaced crowds
    When we are out of the drought?

Food

Warm deliciousness
Familiar wonderful smells
    The crunch
    The chew
The satisfaction of this brain food
It may not be good for your body food

But
    I
        Don't
            Care

The teeth sink
The exquisite taste
I love the triangular slice of circle
    The cheese
    The topping
    The sauce
All combines to my favorite food

Can
    I
        Make
          This
            At
              Home?

Music

Pounding drums
Echoing factories
Calming, soothing sounds

Lyrics lovingly
Caress ears
Buzzing, vibrating chest

Outside world
Shut away
Pounding, echoing drums

Death

Grieving impacts the living
They march on as knowing
      Knowing that their time may come next
Surviving the loss of someone whom you loved
Loved and will miss while you draw breath

What is my impact?
How will I be seen?
Are the thoughts that resonate
      When reading their obituary
         Or writing as the case may be

Who will miss me?
Who will be at my funeral?
Who will help carry me?
Who will sing at my funeral?

Who has loved me?

Papers

Words printed on paper
Meanings derived from within
Did the author mean this?
Did the author mean that?

A professor spoke about meeting one
An author about whom he wrote papers
The author did not appreciate said papers
The professor laughed this to us
        "This is what I do. I write papers."

A literature major
        I wrote papers
Primarily on authors who were dead
        And I wrote
The author meant this
The author meant that
While asking myself,
"Did they really mean this?
Did they really mean that?"

Puppy

Big paws
Soft fur
Jumping machine
Long walk
Still energized

Food whining
Scrap begging
Laying down
At feet
Somewhat calm

Can I afford one?
Will I remember to walk it?
Can I feed it?
Will my apartment allow it?

Innocence

Smiling through my tears
Such innocence laughing
    As dirt covers what remains
    Knowing that all our fears
    Have finished and realized

    The thorn in his side is gone
    The father called him home
I'm happy to know that a new innocence
    Can laugh while the adults mourn

When will his innocence be lost?
How can I stop it?
How can I delay it?
    May he not know this grief for decades
    and decades

Walking

Clean blue shoes
Laced tight around my feet
A steady pace
No one willing to race

A casual stroll around
Late at night
Flashlights on belt loops
And people playing hoops

Three in a party
Challenges going down
Battles being fought
And Pokemon being caught

Following the routes
Can I make one?
What level do I have to be?
Oh, can I see?

Laundry

A pile of them
      Worn and dirty
Work clothes
      Lounge clothes
Higher than my raised bed
      Neatly laid across each other
Spilling over the ripped netted hamper
      Socks balled in bunches
Lying on nearby floor
      Energy to do this none
Despite a dire need for some
      When will energy come?
When will my hangers be full?

Love

Sleeping lonely again
Waiting for love to begin
How will we meet?
Will his eyes be dark like chocolate
Or light like mine?
Will I ever call him mine?

Prayers unsaid and seemingly unanswered
What path will my life lead?
Is there romantic love? I plead
Will he be taller than my family?
How will they interact?
Does he like kids?
I want four
Will I be able to have kids at all?

Sleeping lonely
Staring forlornly
Thoughts racing around
Hopes brought to the ground
Will I ever really be in love?

Homework

When will this happen?
Diligently completing
All of my homework

Book

Why did I do this?
I signed up to write some poems
Not publishing them

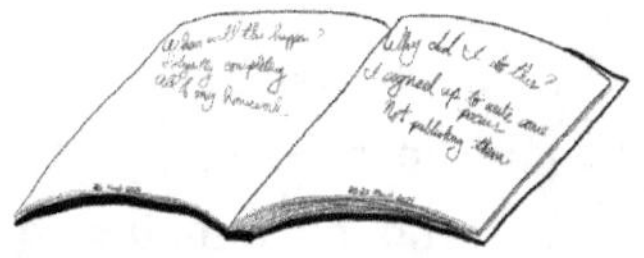

Children

Crying
       Sobbing really
Tears forced down so they don't see them
Sitting
       Hiding really
At a group where the ones who caused it won't
see

A bad night before
       Turned into an awful morning
              Turned into an okay day
Full of laughter
And the traditional headaches
       Then the change
              And the nightmare came again

Why do they treat me this way?
Why do I take it?
Will I leave and never go back?
Should I have called in sick today?

Hardcore

What does hardcore mean?
Is it faithfully dedicated as a fan?
Does it mean only listening to hard rock?
Does it mean going to jail?
Does it mean joining a gang?
What does it mean?

Lights

Multicolored lights
      Shine
Through my closed blinds
The rotating lights even smaller
      On my white wall

Dogs barking
Marking their territory
      To these invaders
A roar of an engine
      But the lights continue

What has caused these lights to stay?
Why have we chosen the colors we have?
Why were the dogs silent for several minutes?
Will I ever know?

Moving

How will he react?
Will he be glad that I'm leaving?
Will it be bittersweet?
Will he be angry that I didn't tell him before?

How will I pay for this?
How will I survive?
Will I be better to my new roommates?
Or will I sink lower into my self-imposed
isolation?

Will I make them cry like she does?
Will I make them angry like she does?

Will I be better there than here?
How will moving go?
Will my summer paychecks cover enough?
Can I afford a car and this?

Sibling

I'm an awful sibling
As the evil little sister
      I know this
But I do love my biological sibling
Even if sometimes we really don't like each
other
      Or talk to each other
      Or use their spouse to bridge our gaps
And communication deficiencies

And watching as the offer of a hug
That hasn't included punches or injury
      since we were minors
Causes them to reluctantly open their arms

Will I ever bridge the ever-widening chasm
between us?
Or will their child be that bridge with their
spouse?
Will they ever be proud of me?
Will they ever answer my fucking texts or calls?
Will I ever stop being looked at as only the evil
little sister?

Commute

Pink clouds
      Brushed on the sky
   Masterfully painted
 Each stroke visible against the deepening blue
sky
They meet the reddish-gray mass on the horizon
The mountains proudly stand tall
Indistinct in the nearing twilight

Red light trios greet me
      on the hot morning beverage road
        over the still wet river

View

Abandoned cars
on forgotten tracks
No graffiti even
on these lingering husks

Seen only by passengers' gazes
If looking to the correct window
Most are too busy
dealing with their lives
because they don't stop
even though you're travelling

The view
       unparalleled
if heartbreaking
due to
       abandoned cars
              on forgotten tracks

Sun-

Sun rise painted water colors across the morning
sky
Sun set fades them away
Every one painted new
Then wiped away by night
Which paints a darker-hued picture
       only illuminated
           by a reflection
              of the painter
                 of the morning
       sky

Faith

Like basking in the sunshine on my face
your love shines down on me
Tears streaming down my face
your love shines all around me

Waiting in silence
closing my eyes
breathing in your love
feeling always your love

thank you for showing me
thank you for telling me
thank you for loving me
thank you for loving me

Lightning

A fire haze descends
   wind blowing
      bad air results

The pass closed to wreck
     then escort because CalTrans fire

Lightning in the mountains
      Will another fire come?
      Will it throw us back into drought?
Lightning in the mountains
      How will we be able to breathe?

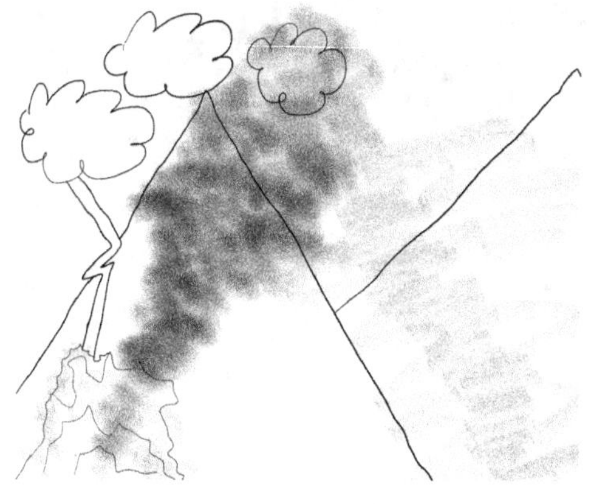

Swift

How does she do it?
Crafting words and melodies
That haunt me in my dreams
    and all my waking hours
Earworms echolessly repeating in my head

How does she do it?
Play an over three-hour show
Multiple nights in a row
Rain pouring down
The crowd chanting more

How does she do it?
My brain asks itself as I connect another line
To a different song
Studying her poetry
And its beautiful
    frightful
        symmetry

Sports?

What is so different about me?
Is it my eyes, my nails, my hands?
Is it because my hair is long?
No, not the hair because your hair can be long
too
and my hair short.
Is it because you have different-lettered
chromosomes
to my twinned ones?
Is it because I have a vagina?
Is it because I have breasts (or will have them)?
Is it because you feel like I'm encroaching on
YOUR sport?
Is it because I have more skill than you?

Missing

Sitting in a dark, empty house
feeling a little maudlin,
a little blue
on the couch you bought
wondering what it's like there

what was it like entering it?
is it as perfect as the Book says it is?
did you have your five people?
was one of them Nana?

I'm praying for a little strength
for a little guidance
what should I do?

Thirst

The mighty Colorado
Succumbed to California's thirst
So too did many other natural bodies of water
found within
Desalination plants redone
Desalination of the ocean,
Attempt to slake Califonria's thirst
The Delta, known for beaching whales and
dolphins, is high
No use of is this water to slake this thirsty state
Much of the thirst goes to farmland
The rest of this goes to the thirsty people
Thirsty people make up the Golden State.
First thirst for land
       Then thirst for gold
              Then thirst for work
                     Now thirst for water
Will anything slake California's thirst?

Starlights

bluffs overlook the city lights and oil fields
the lights shining like grounded stars
drawing a ponderous gaze to them
the rigs distort from the rolling hills
        nearby the Sierra Nevadas
           loom to the east

wet black asphalt draws my gaze
        below my sneakers
fresh from a sprinkling rain
        enough to irritate
not enough for clean air

behind is the college
before is uncertainty
        a new place, a new town, a new life?

It is night
It is dark
only these city lights like guiding stars
moving me forward
pondering what is meant to be

www.ingramcontent.com/pod-product-compliance
Lightning Source LLC
La Vergne TN
LVHW010844200726
843508LV00012B/2743